NORWICH
IN OLD PHOTOGRAPHS

NORWICH
IN OLD PHOTOGRAPHS

COLLECTED BY
MICHAEL COLMAN

ALAN SUTTON

Alan Sutton Publishing Limited
Phoenix Mill · Far Thrupp · Stroud · Gloucestershire

First published 1990

British Library Cataloguing in Publication Data

Colman, Michael
Norwich in old photographs.
1. Norfolk, Norwich, history
I. Title
942.615

ISBN 0–86299–802–6

DEDICATION

This book is dedicated to the memory of George Swain, who took many of the
pictures within.

Typeset in 9/10 Korinna.
Typesetting and origination by
Alan Sutton Publishing Limited.
Printed in Great Britain by
Dotesios Printers Limited.

CONTENTS

UNTHANK ROAD C. 1905.

INTRODUCTION

Birmingham has ten houses. London has only twenty thousand inhabitants, and York, Lincoln and Norwich are the largest towns in England, whose total population stands at around 1-and-a-quarter million. It is January 1067, and William the Conqueror, weeks after his victory at Hastings and only days after his Christmas Day coronation at Westminster Abbey, is standing atop the castle mound amidst the blackened ruins of the wooden fortress he had ordered to be built only weeks before, burnt down by the citizens of the city he now surveys. Around him unfolds the township of Norwich, with some 1,000 humble dwellings and around 5,500 citizens. There is no cathedral: in its place stands the palace of Gyrth Godwinsson, Earl of East Anglia, killed at Hastings along with his brother, King Harold.

Through the town winds the river Wensum which had once provided access for the Saxon invaders who settled at Conesford and Coslany, and later the Danes, whose settlement was at Westwic. The history of Norwich had perhaps begun even earlier, however, when Queen Boudicca built her Iceni palace, three miles south of the site of today's city, during her rebellion against the Romans who had settled at *Venta Icenorum* near Caistor. Following the Roman evacuation of Britain the Saxons invaded in 425, and in East Anglia there was constant conflict between them and the inhabitants of *Northwic*. Four hundred years later in 865 the Danes launched a formidable invasion, and in 869, Edmund, the young king of East Anglia, was tied to a tree and shot to death with arrows.

Norwich was plundered, sacked and burnt by the notorious King Swein (the swine!) in 1004, and the Normans invaded in 1066. This did not deter King Swein, who in 1069 sent a fleet of around 270 ships along the Wensum, and Norwich was sacked once again, only to be beseiged in a rebellion against William six years later. By 1085 the town was dominated by a timber fortress, which two years later was seized and held for three months by the wife of the Earl of East Anglia, whose husband had fled after his involvement in a plot against William the Conqueror.

An era of building began with the commencement of the cathedral in 1096. During a pause in its construction in 1120 the castle keep was begun, and that year Henry I made a Christmas visit to the city, whose population was now approaching 10,000. More stone buildings were beginning to appear: the bishop's palace, and later the fine houses of wealthy merchants.

King Stephen became involved in the story of St William of Norwich when in 1137 the Jewish community, it is said, crucified an innocent little boy in a city house and hung his body from a tree in Thorpe Wood. The king heard matters relating to the incident but deferred action to a general council that brought no charges. Many Norwich Jews were massacred in 1190 when throughout England those preparing for the crusade to Jerusalem decided first to vent their aggression on the English Jews.

The city was again attacked, captured and pillaged in 1174, this time by the forces of the young King Louis, who seized the castle and carried away large sums of money. The raising of cash by Kings could take surprising forms; after the battle of Agincourt Henry V pawned his coronet to the city of Norwich for 1,000 marks. It was kept in a chest in the cathedral priory until redeemed some seven years later. Another way of raising money was to sell certain rights of self government, and Norwich's first 'charter' was granted by Henry II in 1158, followed by a more explicit charter in 1194.

In 1266 Simon de Montford's rebellious barons raided Norwich after losing the civil war at the Battle of Evesham, cutting church bell-ropes so alarms could not be sounded and then sacking the city, killing and kidnapping many citizens. The story of violence seems continuous: six years later, in 1272, trouble broke out between the cathedral monks and the citizens when a brawl began in Tombland resulting in the deaths of several citizens. After barricading themselves inside the close and shooting at anyone who came near, the prior sent for mercenaries from Yarmouth, who swept into the city, burning, pillaging and killing. In retaliation the citizens destroyed the cloisters and fire-bombed other buildings. The rioting became so severe that Henry III had to come in person to restore order, and had thirty citizens who had plundered the priory dragged to death by horses, while others were hanged, drawn, and quartered. As a punishment, the citizens were ordered to build a new gate, St Ethelbert's gate, which still stands in Tombland.

Not surprisingly the defence of the city was becoming a priority, and in 1297 the city wall was begun, taking forty years to complete. The citizens grumbled: free access to the city was now restricted to entrance through gates where a toll had to be paid. The wall was ready in 1349, but five years later it was unable to keep out the invasion of black rats which brought the Black Death to the city; two thousand died, shops and stalls collapsed from disuse, and four parish churches ceased to function entirely, having neither clergy nor parishioners. Following famine and further plagues, the resulting depression led the peasants to rise against the tyranny of their masters in 1381, when under Litster they seized the city, killed the mayor, and governed the county until the rebellion was eventually crushed.

At the end of the 1300s there was a Flemish immigration into Norwich, at a time when the wool trade was growing and the first worsted cloth was being produced. Violence was never far away though: in 1427 the first Wycliffite heretics were burnt in the city and in 1443 the citizens overran the Guildhall and stole the common seal in a dispute over rights.

When Henry VI came to Norwich in 1449 it was a city becoming dominated by rich merchants, and also by the Church; the city was now acquiring its wealth of medieval churches, of which thirty-one still remain today. The early sixteenth century was a period of unemployment and economic decline, when the city became squalid and overcrowded. The many poor were becoming tired of their serfdom, and increasingly irritated by the abuses of the gentry. These with other grievances led to Kett's rebellion, when an army of up to 16,000 Norfolk citizens captured Norwich and attempted to take over the government of the county, but which resulted in the cold blooded massacre of some 3,500 rebels.

Queen Elizabeth I came to Norwich in 1578, a time when a second wave of Flemish immigrants was beginning; soon over a third of the city's 16,000 population were 'strangers'. The city was now 'swarming with tramps' and by the end of the century four-fifths of the city's inhabitants were poor or destitute. Puritanism appeared in Norwich in about 1580, and thirty-two citizens of Norfolk and Norwich sailed on the *Mayflower* in 1620, but the effects of the Reformation on the city were minimal, although some churches were destroyed, and in 1645 the cathedral was sacked and pillaged.

By 1649 when Charles I was deposed, Norwich was a city of 25,000 inhabitants rivalled in size only by Newcastle and Bristol, but the population was reduced by the great plague in 1665 when many Norwich citizens were saved from starving only by a timely glut of herring. The first Norwich newspaper appeared in 1701 and the first bank in 1756, and by 1783 the city was listed as having over 300 shops.

Norwich in 1800 was a city of narrow, crooked streets, some lit by oil lamps and some cobbled, but most simply of compacted earth. The railway arrived in 1844, and as the townspeople moved out to the new outskirts so the country people moved in, to an increasingly dilapidated and depressed city. By 1848 a fifth of the population were paupers, and the textile industry was in decline.

Brewing, and the manufacture of shoes were beginning to replace the old industry; nearly two thousand were now employed in the growing shoe trade. Efforts were being made to clean up the city's image, and in 1853 a committee was formed to organize lighting, paving, cleansing and sanitizing the streets. By 1864 some three thousand city houses had water-closets, although these all emptied into the Wensum which became seriously polluted.

Horse buses began in 1879, and by now Norwich had three stations. Trams were introduced in 1900 and in their first week carried nearly one million passengers.

The First World War emptied Norwich of its menfolk when they rushed to enlist at the opening of hostilities, and of the 100,000 Norfolk men who went to war, 12,000 did not return. The destruction of the city centre and many other parts of the city during the last war imposed new peaks of devastation that it seems Norwich has had to bear many times over its fifteen-hundred-year history; repeatedly attacked, sacked, besieged, captured, pillaged and burnt, the story of Norwich accurately reflects the violent and turbulent history of the English nation.

The City Centre

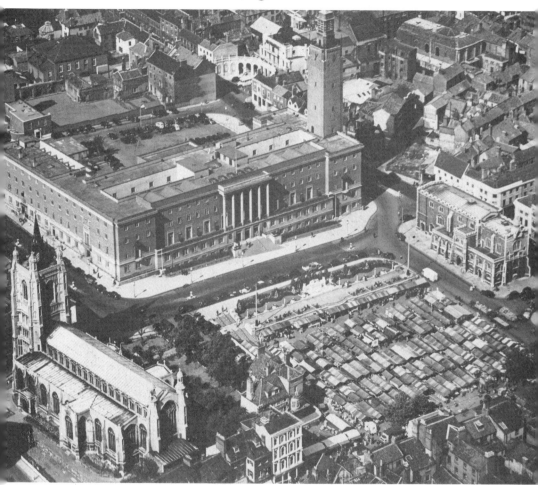

LOOKING DOWN UPON A THOUSAND YEARS OF NORWICH HISTORY c. 1952, with the market place framed on the left by the mighty tower of the five hundred-year-old St Peter Mancroft, in the centre by the imposing face of the City Hall, and on the right by the Guildhall, built nearly six hundred years ago. Queen Elizabeth I and Oliver Cromwell were both visitors to the Guildhall. To the left of the City Hall clock-tower is the Hippodrome, now the site of the St Giles Street multi-storey car park, and between the City Hall and the Guildhall the top of Upper and Lower Goat Lane is still a bomb site.

THE MARKET PLACE in the early 1850s, when St Peter Mancroft had neither 'pepperpots' nor modern spire. At this time Norwich was converting from oil to gas lamps, and the city's first gas lamp, the 'gasolier', is just discernable in the foreground. The building on the left with the bay window is now the Sir Garnet Wolseley pub, but all the buildings to the right of it have been demolished.

THE SAME SITE as above c. 1857. There are now about two hundred stalls on the market but it has not always thrived. In 1544 it had become so overgrown with weeds that a man had to be paid to clear it.

WAITING IN THE WALK — hackney carriages by the cabbie shelter in Gentleman's Walk in 1885.

LITTLE SEEMS TO HAVE CHANGED by 1905 when this picture was taken. The lamps around Wellington have gone but so have the hackney carriages. Tramlines can be seen along the Walk and the decline in horse-drawn transport had begun.

THE MARKET in about 1897. Norwich market was originally at Tombland, which was a convenient place of trade between the nearby Saxon and Danish settlements. When the Normans came they set up their own market on the present site, and entry to it was gained through a toll-house which stood on the site of the Guildhall.

THE STATUE OF THE DUKE OF WELLINGTON erected in 1854, originally stood in the market opposite Davey Place. It now stands in the Upper close and is probably pictured here during removal in 1937. The passer-by at the foot of the picture could not resist a peep.

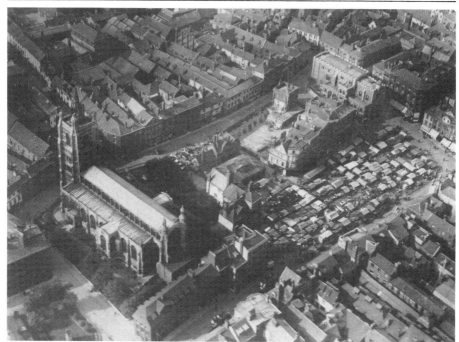

A WARREN OF STREETS AND YARDS stand in 1937 on the site where the city hall was shortly to be built. At the back of the market plans for its expansion have begun with the demolition of the old municipal buildings.

A LONE POLICEMAN POSES FOR THE CAMERA in an eerily empty market place during the 1930s, with the municipal buildings behind him. By now becoming infested with rats, the buildings were shortly to be demolished.

FORCED LABOUR of 'workmen, citizens and foreigners' was used to build the Guildhall. It was begun in 1407 and the east face, with its spectacular flintwork, was carved from Mousehold flint. There were once two towers, but they collapsed in 1508. The clock and turret were added in 1850.

THE VAULTS OF THE GUILDHALL were used as a prison from 1412, and in 1549 Kett the rebel was imprisoned there before his execution. Shown here in the 1890s is Guildhall Hill, recently pedestrianized, and perhaps not too soon. Even in 1795 the city authorities had been urged 'to bring to justice the young men who endangered life by driving carts furiously up and down Gaol Hill'.

SANDBAGGED AND BOARDED UP in the expectation of war in 1939, and yet in 1908 the Guildhall was saved from demolition only by the casting vote of the mayor. The seat of the city government for over five hundred years, 529 successive mayors and lord mayors presided here. Only twenty years after its completion in 1433, the mayor was imprisoned for his part in an incident when the citizens of Norwich surged into the building and ran off with the common seal. During Litster's Rebellion of 1381, the city of Norwich was seized and the mayor killed.

'THE BEST ICE CREAM ON THE MARKET' reads the sign on the barrow at the bottom of the picture, but the top stall also advertises theirs as 'best on market'. Perhaps the first stall has the business edge, having ice-cream 'made by electricity'! This view was taken in 1922, with a Model T Ford descending Guildhall Hill.

ONLOOKERS at the demolition of the old municipal buildings, pulled down in 1937.

RE-LAYING THE MARKET PLACE during its expansion in 1938. The market was paved with wooden blocks in 1874 after a successful experiment in London Street, and soon most city streets were paved in this way.

A BUSY SCENE IN THE WALK, C. 1915, as tram No. 25 to Earlham Road and Thorpe Road rounds the corner into Guildhall Hill. Gentleman's Walk was the only paved street in the city in 1800, when the walk on a market day was 'thronged with a collection of very interesting characters: the merchant, the manufacturer, the magistrate, the provincial yeoman, the militia officer, the affluent landlord, the thrifty and thriving tenant, the independent farmer, the recruiting officer, the clergy, faculty, barristers, and all the various characters of polished and professional society'. There were about 300 shops in the city at that time, and the streets were mostly crooked and narrow, according to their medieval pattern. Lit by some 900 oil lamps, those not cobbled with sea-shore flints were simply of compacted earth.

NOTHING WAS DEMOLISHED for the building of the Royal Arcade; it was simply cut through the house with the balconies on the right, shown here in the 1890s. Said to be 'perfectly innocent in the front but very naughty when its back is turned', the Arcade, with its art nouveau tilework, was designed by Skipper and opened in 1899. On the far left is Davey Place. Davey, an extreme radical, joked he would make a hole in the king's head: he subsequently bought the inn of that name, knocked it down, and created the street that bears his name.

HAY HILL in 1854, taken from about the same angle as the picture at the top of the opposite page. At this time the White Horse on the left was gabled, but the Barley Mow behind it, although later the Cambridge, looks just the same in both pictures.

HACKNEY CARRIAGES AND CARRIERS' CARTS on Hay Hill in 1881, the year extensive repairs had to be carried out to St Peter Mancroft, and its 'pepperpots' were added. The building on the right is still there today, in modified form, but all the others have been demolished.

NORWICH CABBIES POSE FOR THE CAMERA c. 1890, pictured from the Haymarket looking into Hay Hill, with the White Horse on the right. In 1880 there were about ten shops here selling 'clothes, brushes, baskets, cheese, china and other commodities'.

NOT ONE BUILDING REMAINS to recall the grandeur of the Haymarket after the devastation of the Second World War. Above, c. 1985, a cobbled Hay Hill leads onto the Haymarket where a policeman stands outside the Savings Bank at the entrance to Little Orford Street. Below, in the 1960s, the International stands on the left, Pilch's in the centre, and Peter Robinson occupies the site to the right.

KNIGHTED BY CHARLES II IN ST ANDREWS HALL, Sir Thomas Browne, whose statue, pictured here in 1965, stands on Hay Hill, was an eminent physician who lived and practised medicine in a house nearby from 1637 until 1682. After his death his skull was sold to a Norwich doctor, kept in a museum for eighty years, and then replaced in his grave in 1922.

THE MOST IMPRESSIVE PARISH CHURCH IN NORFOLK, St Peter Mancroft is shown here in 1870 before its modern spire was added. It was built in 1403, replacing an earlier church whose churchyard had to be extended after the ravages of the Black Death in 1349, when a third of the city's 6,000 residents died, and further plagues in 1361 and 1369. Three hundred years earlier, after the Norman Conquest, an influx of immigrants settled here in a large field or *Magna Crofta*, which became known as Mancroft.

ST PETER'S STREET in the 1930s, with the west wall of the Guildhall showing on the left, and a Hudson motor car parked on the right outside the later site of the city hall. It was from a shop here that John Smith began to make and sell ready-made shoes in 1792 and started an industry that by 1935 employed twelve thousand people.

A FIRE BRIGADE DISPLAY AT THE CITY HALL, 1855, seen from St Peter Mancroft. Looking at the figure at the top of the ladder, one hopes the fire brigade were soon able to improve their methods!

THE FISHMARKET pictured here in 1900, was built to replace the earlier 'stinking, ramshackle, canvas market'. The cart on the left, outside the site of the city hall, is being emptied of its load of large china bowls, and on the right is the Fishmongers Arms.

A CLOSE UP VIEW OF THE FISHMONGERS ARMS, which stood on the site of today's memorial gardens, where, coincidentally, people still gather today to eat their fish and chips bought at the market.

THE BEE HIVE PUBLIC HOUSE once stood on the site of the City Hall, and is pictured here from the Guildhall in about 1930. It was demolished in 1937.

ST PETER MANCROFT in the 1930s, photographed from the courtyard of The White Swan inn, which stood on the site of today's Shoppers' Car Park.

THE CORNER OF BETHEL STREET and St Peter's Street in 1961, showing the premises of James Wones, fruit merchants, and the warehouse of Buntings, whose shop stood on the site of today's Marks and Spencer.

THE SHOPPERS' CAR PARK in 1972, with the west wall of St Peter's on the left. Comparison of this wall with the top photograph shows that unbelievably one is looking at the same spot only eleven years apart.

BETHEL STREET in the 1920s, seen through the railings of St Peter's. On the right is the Mancroft restaurant, now the site of the police station and City Hall.

THE WHEATSHEAF, No. 14 Bethel Street, in 1935 after it had ceased trading. The old saying goes that Norwich has a pub for every day of the year. There are actually about twice that number.

BETHEL STREET WAS NAMED AFTER THE BETHEL STREET HOSPITAL, founded in 1713 'for the habitation of poor lunatics, and not for natural-born fools or idiots'.

THE FIRE STATION now stands where these gabled houses stood in 1920, when this photograph was taken. Opposite is the site of today's library, and in the background stands St Peter's. They say that the city has a church for every Sunday, but the figure is again about twice that number.

TWO PICTURES TAKEN FROM THE SAME VIEWPOINT in 1960 and below, 1975. On the left in the top picture is Buntings Warehouse, and next door is the headquarters of the Norwich Civil Defence. Beyond lie Future Stores and The Gardeners Store, while the house on the right with the two chimneys, above the boy on the bicycle, is where the library was later built. Car enthusiasts might like to spot the Morris 8 open tourer and the two Ford 10s.

THE LIBRARY WAS OPENED by the Queen Mother in 1963, and one of the streets that was demolished to make way for it was Lady Lane, birthplace of Richard Hearne, TV's 'Mr Pastry'.

RAMPANT HORSE STREET in 1965, with the wall of St Stephen's church on the left providing an accurate point of comparison with the 1975 picture below. Taking its name from a pub which once stood here, it leads into Theatre Street, named after Thomas Ivory's theatre of 1758, which had previously been known as Chapel Field Lane.

RAMPANT HORSE STREET C. 1850, presenting a picturesque scene. Not one of these buildings remains, except St Stephen's church, where three of the author's ancestors, all Sheriffs of Norwich, lie buried.

BEDECKED WITH BUNTING, Rampant Horse Street during the Jubilee of 1935. Buntings' store is on the left, on the present site of Marks and Spencer. Parked outside is the forerunner of all Jaguar cars, an SSI, then produced by a firm of motor cycle manufacturers. Looking across, a Singer Junior makes its way along the street, and to its right is an Austin Seven and behind it, a Morris Cowley.

ST STEPHEN'S STREET in 1961, with the Great Eastern public house, popular with the railwaymen, at the corner of St Stephen's Road and Queen's Road.

THE SCENE IN ST STEPHEN'S STREET, around 1908. On the right are the premises of Percy Bush, 'Artistic Hairdresser', and next door the sign hanging outside Lambert's advertises their tea. Further down at the junction of Surrey Street stands the thatched Boar's Head Inn, built in 1495 and destroyed by the *Luftwaffe* in 1942.

THE DECEMBER DISPLAY AT YALLOPS in St Stephen's, c. 1930. At that time onions were a penny a pound, potatoes 2d., sprouts 3d., grapes 7d., brazil nuts 8d., and apples five for 3d.

THE RED LION TOBACCO STORES, No. 8 Red Lion Street, which stood at the corner of Back Rampant Horse Street. Shown in around 1895, when Nelson cigarettes cost 6d. a packet and Key West cigars were 2d. each, or seven for 1s.

THE VIEW FROM ST STEPHEN'S PLAIN along Red Lion Street in 1887, with the site of Debenhams on the left and a glimpse of the castle in the background. These buildings were pulled down during road widening in 1900 for the introduction of trams. A new row of buildings was erected, designed by Skipper, architect of the Royal Arcade.

CURLS AND THEN DEBENHAMS STOOD ON THIS SITE, pictured here in the 1890s when Miss Harcourt's, whose window on the left was filled with large-brimmed hats, stood next to R. Curry's 'Harness Manufactory'.

A CAR PARK AT CURLS in 1952, after the store had been destroyed by bombs in the Norwich blitz of 1942, showing a mixture of the cars of the period: Morrisses, Wolseleys, Hillmans etc. On the far right is the Coach and Horses and on the left the Cricketers' Arms.

AN ATMOSPHERIC VIEW of Little Orford Street in 1895, pictured from the Haymarket. The site of today's Pilch's store is on the right, and in the centre background the Goose and Grid Iron stands at the junction of Back Rampant Horse Street, now the site of Debenhams.

LITTLE ORFORD STREET in 1895, photographed from outside the Goose and Grid Iron, shown in the above picture. The Savings Bank is at the top of the street on the right, and in Brigg Street are the London restaurant and Liptons, seen in previous photographs of the Haymarket area. Little Orford Street was demolished in 1901.

A CLOSE-UP VIEW OF THE GOOSE AND GRID IRON, shown on the previous page, in 1895. The area was demolished to make Orford Place, and was later the site of Curls and then Debenhams. In about 1883 Norwich had 536 inns, hotels and taverns, and some 75 'beer houses'.

COLLINS AND SHORTEN'S INDIA RUBBER WAREHOUSE, Orford Place, in the 1920s, when it seems one could not only hire a waterbed but have one's suction hose delivered!

TRAM NO. 39 TO CITY ROAD makes its way past the Cricketers' Arms in Red Lion Street, c. 1905.

ORFORD PLACE in the early 1930s with Curls on the left, and on the right, standing over Burlington Buildings, a tower which provides a useful reference point with the earlier photograph opposite. Once the old Jewish quarter and the site of the earliest known herb garden in England, Orford Place has seen constant rebuilding through the years, being known variously as Orford Street, Great Orford Street, Little Orford Street, and Rampant Horse Lane. The confusion still exists today.

THE VIEW FROM ORFORD HILL in 1928. Tram No. 47 on the right meets tram No. 4 to Magdalen Road, while parked in the foreground are a Morris 8 fabric saloon, a 1927 Humber and a 1928 Morris Cowley.

THE BELL HOTEL looking brand new in 1895. Outside the entrance stands the hotel's own carriage.

ORFORD HILL FROM THE BELL HOTEL, 1895, with Boston's house furnishers on the left, and Collins and Shorten at the junction of Orford Place.

BOSTON'S LATER MOVED into this unusual cast-iron and glass-fronted building in Market Avenue, built c. 1868 and formerly the premises of Messrs Pank.

THE NOTORIOUS HELL-FIRE CLUB used to meet at the Bell in the eighteenth century, with the avowed intention of 'destroying the Methodists'. It is shown here c. 1895 when it was evidently possible to drive a coach and horses straight through the entrance and out the other side.

ORFORD HILL in the 1960s. William Clarke's on the left has gone, demolished in 1900 to make way for the Castle Meadow tram track.

THE FRONT AND BACK OF WILLIAM CLARKE'S C. 1895, just prior to its demolition for the Castle
Meadow tram track.

THE YORK TAVERN, seen on the left, stood in Castle Meadow opposite the Bell Hotel. Pictured here in about 1895, on the left is the short alley-way that still connects to White Lion Street.

THE CASTLE DITCH, later Castle Meadow was dug by the Normans as part of the original timber castle's fortifications and eventually became a narrow lane that ended at the Bell Hotel. Filled in and widened in 1900 for the coming of the trams, there was still barely room for two trams to pass.

CASTLE MEADOW in 1924 showing Opie Street, once known as Devil's Alley, on the right.

CASTLE MEADOW, 1924, with Opie Street on the right, where the novelist Amelia Opie lived until her death in 1853. Sister of Harriet Martineau and wife of John Opie the portrait painter, she became the darling of society in Norwich and London, and counted Sheridan, Byron and Wordsworth among her acquaintances.

LADIES' HEMLINES WERE RISING for the first time in 1905 when this photograph of London Street was taken. Feet became visible, but definitely not the ankles. An ornamental hat was the height of fashion, and within a few years women were wearing extraordinarily wide hats, the brims sometimes exceeding the width of the shoulders. Wasp waists were going out of fashion and waistlines, usually marked by a ribbon sash, were rising. London Street has always been one of the busiest in the city, and used to be one of the narrowest until it was

widened in 1856. Kerbed and laid with flagstones in 1863, it was experimentally paved with wooden blocks in 1874, and after a successful trial other city streets were paved in this way. It was widened to its present width of 20 ft in 1876. Cars started to appear on Norwich roads at the start of the century, and in 1903 the speed limit was raised to 20 m.p.h. The car on the right of the picture could be a Montant-Brouillet, but is probably a Renault. Can anyone say for sure?

A BOMB INTENDED FOR THE CITY HALL, it was said, destroyed the Cloverleaf Café, which stood here between Upper and Lower Goat Lane. Although still a bomb site when it was photographed from the City Hall clock tower in about 1950, a novel use seems to have been found for it by advertising air-tours of Norfolk. 'Book Here, Book Now' read the placards under the wing, and a group of passers-by consider just that.

HARDYMENTS of St Giles Street, the 'noted house for dinner, tea and toilet sets' in about 1936. In their window stands a display of Decoro pottery, mostly jugs and jars selling at 9s. 6d.

THE TOP OF GUILDHALL HILL, with the site of the City Hall on the right, pictured c. 1936. The Guildhall is just visible over the houses on the extreme left.

UNTHANK ROAD AND ST GILES GATES, as they were in the 1930s, now better known as the corner of Earlham Road and Unthank Road, at their junction by the Roman Catholic church, seen on the left. Today a pedestrian flyover straddles Grapes Hill and the top of Wellington Lane, which can be seen emerging between the hotel on the left and the two advertisements for Bovril and Capstan.

THE ROMAN CATHOLIC CHURCH OF ST JOHN THE BAPTIST, popularly known as the Roman Catholic cathedral, at the junction of Unthank Road and Earlham Road, pictured in 1950 before the Grapes Hill improvements. Financed by the Duke of Norfolk, and completed in 1910, it was built on the site of the Norfolk City Gaol. A regime of silence was enforced at the gaol and two executions took place there: that of William Sheward, wife murderer and landlord of the Key and Castle in Oak Street, and that of Mr Stratford, who poisoned his wife, in 1829.

A TRANQUIL SCENE IN POTTERGATE C. 1925, with Ten Bell Lane on the right and Cow Hill to the left.

ST BENEDICT'S ALLEY in 1937. This old gabled house was demolished the following year. Just visible is the tower of St Benedict's church, all that remains of the one-thousand-year-old building that suffered bomb damage during the war.

BRIDEWELL ALLEY pictured from outside the entrance to the Bridewell Museum, c. 1895. The museum, once the home of William Appleyard, Norwich's first mayor, dates from 1370, but by 1583 it had become a 'bridewell', a prison for tramps and beggars. Its north wall, facing St Andrew's church, is said to be the finest example of squared flintwork in England, and in its vaults the earliest example of the use of brick in Norwich can be seen.

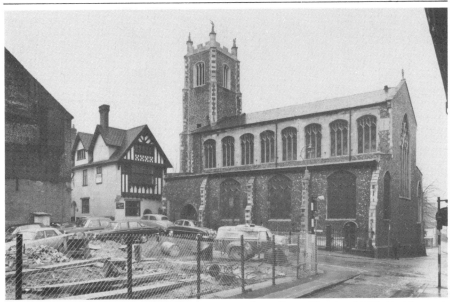

AN UNUSUAL VIEW OF ST JOHN MADDERMARKET, seen from Dove Street c. 1967. Madder roots produce a red dye, and local weavers once bought theirs nearby. During Kett's rebellion of 1549, the Earl of Warwick, having fought his way through St John Maddermarket, was ambushed at St Andrew's Plain and pinned down by a hail of arrows before driving the attack off and pursuing the rebels through the cathedral towards the rebel camp on Mousehold.

THE CORN HALL in 1862, where Liszt once gave a performance and where the great violinist Paganini astounded his audience in 1831, after first flabbergasting them with the price of the tickets. The great Norwich painters used to exhibit here, and many famous boxers, wrestlers and entertainers appeared here too. The Corn Hall was demolished in 1963.

QUEEN ELIZABETH I walked through St John's Alley in August 1578 while on a visit to Norwich and on her way from the Guildhall to the Duke of Norfolk's Palace, which once stood on the site of today's Duke Street multi-storey car park. The alley is pictured here in the 1920s, and below in 1975.

WILL KEMP, the Elizabethan actor, won a bet by Morris dancing from London to Norwich, and finished his nine-day journey with a leap over the churchyard wall of St John's. At the foot of the churchyard still stands the parish water pump, once the sole water supply for the entire parish, the population of which in 1865 still stood at only 537.

UNBELIEVABLY THIS AND THE LOWER PICTURE WERE TAKEN FROM IDENTICIAL VIEWPOINTS only eleven years apart. This was St Andrew's Street and Charing Cross in 1960 and below in 1971. Exchange Street is on the left, and on the right is the old library and Norwich Museum where the Duke of Norfolk's Palace once stood. Unbelievers should compare the upper wall of the electrical shop on the left and the factory chimney, the top of which is visible in the top picture.

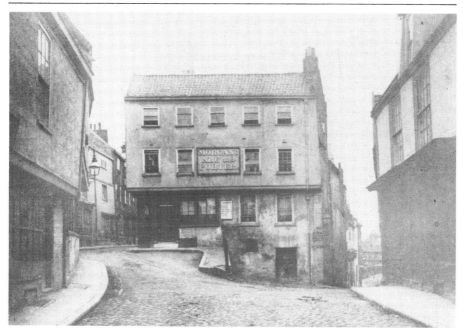

THE THREE PIGEONS, Charing Cross, c. 1865, with St Benedict's Street to the left and Westwick Street on the right. Leaning in from the left is the Strangers' Hall, its frontage dating from 1621. The strangers were Flemish refugees encouraged to settle in the city for their textiles skills. In 1579, more than a third of the city's population of 16,000 were 'strangers'.

THE LORD CAMDEN PUBLIC HOUSE, Charing Cross, in about 1900, with Lord Camden's Yard on the left. Charing Cross was once called Shearer's Cross, but during a craze for naming Norwich streets after those of London, Shearer's Cross, or 'Shearing Cross' became Charing Cross.

BRICK-NOGGING is the name given to brickwork between timber frames, and this house, once the home of an Elizabethan MP and mayor of Norwich, is a fine example. A cinema was later built on the site, and all but the centre structure was demolished. Standing in awkward isolation among faceless modern buildings, it is now the home of the Norwich Telephone Museum. It is pictured here in about 1930.

THE CITY ARMS, on the corner of St Andrew's Street and St Andrew's Hill, a spot better known today for its two telephone boxes. The building to its right still exists, but the house to its left is now the site of a cinema. Photographed here in about 1895, it was demolished in 1899 when St Andrew's was cut through to Redwell Street so that tramlines could be laid.

ST ANDREW'S CHURCH and the corner of Bridewell Alley c. 1895. Its tower dates from 1478, and the church contains the tombs of the Suckling family, and of Bishop Underwood, arch-prosecutor of local heretics during Mary Tudor's reign.

ST BENEDICT'S GATES in the 1930s with Barn Road on the right, before the area was devastated during the last war. The gates were once garlanded with flowers as Queen Elizabeth I passed through at the end of her visit to Norwich in 1578.

BANK STREET c. 1895, looking towards Upper King Street, and about two years before the Royal Hotel was built on the site to the right.

REDWELL STREET, leading to Elm Hill, c. 1895, prior to the making of the cut through to St Andrew's Street in 1899. Number five on the left was then the premises of Charles Payne, gas light specialist, and next door down was the Cabinetmakers' Arms. It has been fascinating to wander around Norwich comparing old photographs and their present locations. It often reveals quirky details: for instance, the Congregational church on the right has to the left of its doorway a notice board stating the times of the services. It is no longer there – but the screw holes still are!

BANK PLAIN in 1938, near the site of today's post office, with Spelmans on the right and outside the Silver Shop next door, a Ford Talbot and, facing it, a Triumph Gloria.

ELM HILL WAS COMPLETELY BURNT DOWN in 1507 and the only building to survive was the King's Arms, later renamed the Briton's Arms, seen to the right. In 1549 the street was the scene of heavy fighting during Kett's rebellion, and four 'gentlemen of the royal army' lie buried in St Simon and St Jude's at the foot of the hill. This photograph was taken c. 1905, when the elm tree shown was still young.

THE MASONIC TAVERN, ELM HILL, c. 1895 with Crown Court on the left. Here was the Strangers' Club where Queen Elizabeth I is said to have watched a pageant in her honour from a window on the first floor. Near the top of the street a plaque marks the home of 'Father Ignatius', who attempted to introduce a new kind of religion in Norwich. His attempts were abandoned in 1866 after a thousand citizens crowded into the street and tried to burn his house down.

TOMBLAND, in 1905. Tombland has nothing to do with tombs; it comes from the Danish word meaning 'open space'. In 1272 it was the scene of serious rioting between monks and citizens, and Henry III had to come in person to restore order.

WENSUM STREET AT THE TURN OF THE CENTURY, with Elm Hill on the left. The Maid's Head Hotel is on the right, where Queen Elizabeth I stayed during her visit to Norwich in 1578; one of the oldest hostelries in England, it dates from about 1287.

TOMBLAND SEEN FROM UPPER KING STREET in the 1890s, when an air of dilapidation is confirmed by a glance at the roof on the left.

AGRICULTURAL HALL PLAIN in about 1905. The hall, now occupied by Anglia TV, was built in 1882 and in its time has seen many uses. Gladstone spoke here and the famous Blondin once led a man across the hall on a tightrope stretched over the heads of the audience. Below it is the old GPO building, once the Crown Bank (1866), and in the distance is Prince of Wales Road, built in 1862 to improve the link between Thorpe station and the city centre.

CATTLE BEING DRIVEN DOWN KING STREET in 1925. Probably Roman in origin, King Street was a street of fashionable houses until the eighteenth century. Further down is the Jacobean façade of the Music House, into which was incorporated Isaac's House, the oldest dwelling in Norwich, built in 1175 by Jurnet and his son Isaac, two of the wealthiest Jews in twelfth-century England.

MURRELL'S YARD, KING STREET, c. 1910, later the location of Ben Burgess Ltd. The Norwich 'yards' were once notorious and often unsanitary, typically with too many families crowded into too few houses.

THE BOILER-MAKERS' ARMS, King Street, in about 1910, when a bottle of Morgan's bottled ale or stout cost 2s. 6d. Fred Marris, landlord c. 1911-14, used to hire out land carts for market traders and commercial travellers.

BER STREET, unusually wide for a Norwich street, is probably Roman in origin. It was once a horse trading centre, and a route for the cattle being driven from the cattlemarket to Trowse. Many of these building were lost during the Second World War when bombs intended for the nearby Thorpe station fell wide of their target. The picture was taken from outside the Jolly Butchers, c. 1925, and shows the church of St Michael at Thorn in the distance.

ALL SAINT'S GREEN in the 1930s, showing the site of today's Bonds store, with Ber Street on the left.

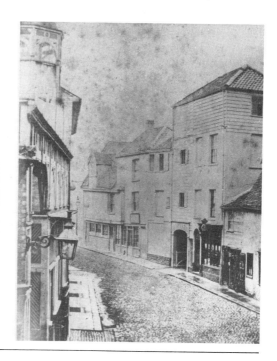

GOLDEN BALL STREET in about 1860. It was named after the Golden Ball public house—the golden ball can just be seen hanging over the far end of the street. The area was well known for its stables, and the entrance to Barnard's stable is on the right. The Pig and Misery Inn stood nearby, one of the notorious pubs of a neighbourhood where spittoons were common and patrons in need of a toilet would use a communal chamber pot kept in a corner of the bar.

GOLDEN BALL STREET in about 1926, when it was still cobbled. The gabled building at the back, destroyed by bombs during the Second World War, is now the site of Bonds.

THE CATTLEMARKET stood on this site, once part of the castle bailey, for three hundred years before it moved in 1960 to the outskirts of the city. The castle, built 1120–30 to replace a timber fortress constructed on the orders of William the Conqueror, has had a fairly uneventful history. Used as the county gaol between 1220 and 1887, public executions were carried out by the gate well into the nineteenth century. One of the last was watched by 11,000 spectators.

ROSE LANE, pictured here in the 1890s, was once the main route to the city centre from Thorpe station. The route was tortuously narrow, across the old Foundry Bridge, and up Rose Lane to the Castle Ditches, later Castle Meadow, and on to the market through Opie Street and London Street, which until widened in 1856, was one of the narrowest streets in the city.

A CONSIGNMENT OF BICYCLES, hauled on LNER carts, halts for the photographer on its way up Prince of Wales Road in the 1920s.

PRINCE OF WALES ROAD in 1974. The road was built in 1860 to better communication between Thorpe station and the city centre. Debris from the old city wall at Chapel Field was used for the foundations.

PRINCE OF WALES ROAD in 1963. On the right is an unusual bus, a Bristol SC fibre-glass bodied saloon, one of only two made.

<u>SECTION TWO</u>

Aviation, Recreation and Sport

HANG ON TO YOUR HATS. The intrepid B.C. Hucks takes off from Hethersett in August 1912, obscuring his assistants who are keeping hold of the tailplane, in a cloud of dust.

THE FIRST RECORDED FLIGHT OVER NORFOLK was made by Bentfield C. Hucks on 10 August 1912, when he flew from Gorleston to Church Lane, Eaton, in a Blériot XI monoplane called *Firefly*. This particular aeroplane, No. 16, had been made in 1909 for the veteran pioneer and aircraft manufacturer Leon Delagrange, and was only the second of this popular model off the production line. Blériot became the first man to fly an aeroplane across the English Channel in 1909, a feat he achieved in $36\frac{1}{2}$ minutes.

BENTFIELD C. HUCKS, upon landing in Norwich, was mobbed by women admirers clamouring for his autograph. At Hethersett in 1914, he became the first British pilot to fly a loop-the-loop.

THE BLÉRIOT XI MONOPLANE had a cruising speed of only 36 m.p.h., dismountable wings for easy transport, and an original asking price of £480. Ailerons were not invented then, and pilots achieved 'balance' by means of a lever which literally 'warped' the wings.

BASED ON THE DESIGN OF A 'SUPER-ZEPPELIN' that had been forced down in 1916, R33 broke away from its mooring on 15 April 1925 and was blown by high winds out over the sea as far as the Dutch coast. The crew managed to lash down the flapping fabric of the nose and bring the airship back to Pulham, where 300 men and boys formed a landing party and successfully brought it back to earth to rousing cheers. King George V later honoured the entire crew with presentation watches.

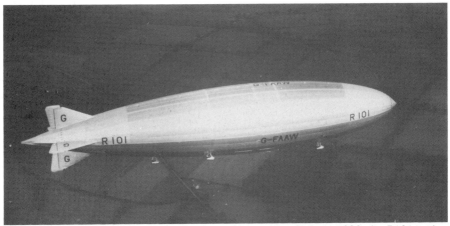

THE LARGEST AIRSHIP IN THE WORLD at the time of its maiden flight in 1930, the R101, with a steel airframe made by Boulton and Paul, had a dining room for fifty persons, a smoking room, and electric kitchens. It set out on its first commercial flight in high winds on 4 October 1930, became crippled, and crashed near Paris, killing 48 of its 54 passengers, among them the air minister.

MPS ABOUT TO BOARD R36 for a trip on 17 June 1921. The Norwich and Norfolk Air Club was formed in 1927, on land previously used by Boulton and Paul at Mousehold.

A PARTY OF NORWICH RADIO DEALERS at Mousehold airfield about to embark on an aircraft bound for Olympia in 1935.

HALF HELICOPTER, HALF AEROPLANE — the autogiro, forerunner of the helicopter, at Heston, 7 January 1930. This Cierva C19 Mk II was 18 ft long, had a four-bladed 30 ft rotor, and had a cruising speed of 70 m.p.h. However, it also had wings, a tailplane and a small engine in the nose.

PRINCE GEORGE, on a visit to Norwich for the boy scout rally in 1933, was due to be escorted in by this Norwich Aero Club aeroplane which ran out of fuel when the prince's flight became overdue.

AMY JOHNSON AT NORWICH, 17 March 1931. Piloting a Gipsy Moth, she became the first woman to fly solo from England to Australia in May 1930. She later made further record breaking flights to Japan and South Africa, but in 1941 her plane ditched into the Thames and she was accidentally killed during the rescue operation.

THE INFLEXIBLE in 1929, the largest monoplane ever to land at Norwich. Its size becomes apparent after a glance at the location of the pilot, whose head can just be seen in the open cockpit.

ANOTHER AIRBORNE PHOTOGRAPHIC EXPEDITION for George Swain, one of the pioneers of aerial photography, who took many of the pictures in this book, with his pilot Frank Neale on the right, in July 1920. Below, George Swain in 1950.

THE PLAYERS AND STAFF OF NORWICH CITY FOOTBALL CLUB at 'The Nest' 1925/6. This was their home from 1907 to 1934.

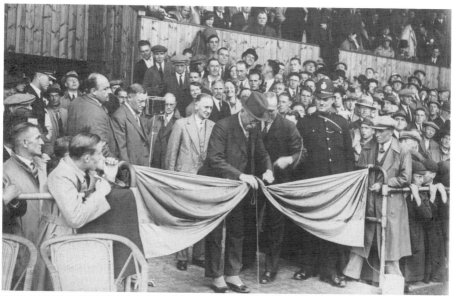

THE OPENING OF CARROW ROAD FOOTBALL GROUND, 1934. The club made its first appearance on 6 September 1902 when they drew 1–1 with Harwich. Norwich's association with 'The Canaries' dates back to the times of the 'Strangers', refugee Flemish immigrants who brought with them their love of gardens and canary breeding.

THE GOTHIC MINSTRELS, all employees of the firm that became Laurence Scott, on an outing to Sandringham. The date of this photograph is uncertain, but a magnifying glass reveals that the car in the centre has exterior tube cooling of a type manufactured in 1903.

THE EAST ANGLIAN CYCLING CLUB in 1921 — its first year of existence. The premises of R.O. Clarke, motor engineer, is on the left.

R.O. CLARKE, the Norwich motor cycle dealer, seen with the Levis motor cycle with which he won the lightweight class of the Junior Tourist Trophy races on the Isle of Man in 1920.

A CAPACITY CROWD at The Firs, the Norwich Speedway, in about 1951.

DON DIMES at the Eastern Speedway, 1929–30.

THE HOME TEAM AT NORWICH SPEEDWAY in 1930. From left to right are Jack Sharpe, Don Dimes, Johnny Bull (captain), Arthur Reynolds (Seated), Bert Peters and Bill Butler.

SECTION THREE

Events

QUEEN VICTORIA'S DIAMOND JUBILEE, 29 July 1897, as the jubilee procession makes its way up Prince of Wales Road. It was not raining, but Victorians had little liking for the sun and parasols were popular for portable shade.

'SURESHOT' – *the leading* 2*d.* smoke, part of the diamond jubilee procession in 1897. Sureshot cigars were certainly popular at this time; advertisements for them appear in photographs of this era throughout the book.

THOUSANDS THRONG THE MARKET PLACE during the diamond jubilee celebrations.

THE UNVEILING OF THE MEMORIAL TO EDITH CAVELL, the Norwich nurse shot by the Germans in 1915 for helping allied prisoners to escape. She was buried in the cathedral close, and this memorial to her in Tombland was unveiled on 12 October 1918.

VOTES FOR WOMEN! Campaigners sell *The Suffragette* in Prince of Wales Road, 13 June 1914, with Mann Egerton's on the right.

EVENING NEWS BOYS OFF TO THE HIPPODROME, 1905. The 'Hooray' seems a little optimistic. Flanked by the two enormous old gas lamps, the boys can hardly raise a smile between them. Is your father or grandfather there?

KING GEORGE VI AND QUEEN ELIZABETH open the City Hall on 29 October 1938.

QUEEN ELIZABETH THE QUEEN MOTHER, at the cathedral in May 1938, flanked by the Dean of Norwich on the right, and the Lord Bishop of Norwich on the left. Queen Elizabeth was there to unveil statuettes of the King and herself in the cathedral cloister.

DAME SYBIL THORNDIKE with the Lord Mayor at the Guildhall on 8 March 1937, while she was appearing at the Theatre Royal.

TESSIE O'SHEA at the Theatre Royal early in 1934.

THE TIME BALL on the castle was first fired on 10 August 1900 and is pictured here during its removal on 6 May 1938.

MARIE LLOYD, the music-hall comedienne, steps into her car after visiting the Heigham Street school during the First World War.

THE STAGE OF THE THEATRE ROYAL after the fire of 22 June 1934. That afternoon an assistant cashier noticed flames underneath the safety curtain and just over two hours later the theatre had been gutted in what was then one of the fiercest fires known in Norwich.

THE BUILDING OF THE BUS STATION, opened 24 March 1936.

THE DEMOLITION OF THE MUNICIPAL BUILDINGS, which stood at the back of the market, in 1937.

SECTION FOUR

Entertainment

THE ELECTRIC THEATRE c. 1913. Popularly known as the Electric Cinema, and later renamed the Norvic, it was the first Norwich cinema to show films in Cinemascope.

THE GRAND OPERA HOUSE pictured after its opening in 1903. The following year the name was changed to the Hippodrome and it became a vaudeville theatre, and later a top variety and music-hall venue. However, its fortunes declined and after a spell as the Norfolk Playhouse it closed in 1960 after fifty-seven years.

THE HIPPODROME pictured from the City Hall clock tower in 1960. The Norfolk Hotel once stood here, a favourite haunt of George Borrow, author of *Lavengro* and *Romany Rye*. It is now the site of the St Giles' Street multi-storey car park.

INSIDE AND OUT in 1960. The interior of the Hippodrome once echoed to the voices of artists such as Laurel and Hardy, Tommy Trinder and Sandy 'Can you hear me mother?' Powell. The acoustics were very good and Lloyd George once complimented the owner on the quality of sound within the theatre.

THE END OF AN ERA. Workmen dismantle the Hippodrome orchestra pit as demolition proceeds. In April 1942 a direct hit from a high explosive bomb blew the stage into the air, but it fell back intact, four inches above its normal level. The stage manager was killed in the blast and so too were three other people, one of them the trainer of a visiting troupe of performing seals.

THE DEMOLITION OF THE HIPPODROME in October 1966, showing the Gladstone Club in the background.

THE STAFF OF THE HIPPODROME line up for the camera in about 1950. Can anyone recall any of their names?

THE HAYMARKET PICTURE HOUSE, now the site of Top Shop, seen from St Peter Mancroft.

OPENING NIGHT AT THE ODEON, 1938, showing *The Sky's The Limit* as its first feature with Mara Loseff and Jade Buchanan.

THE THEATRE ROYAL pictured after its opening in 1935. This was the third theatre to stand on the site. The original theatre, designed by Thomas Ivory, opened in 1758 as 'The Concert Hall', and became the Theatre Royal in 1768. It was later demolished and a new theatre built in 1826, but this was destroyed by fire in 1934. The theatre has seen more famous actors than can be listed, but the most notable was Edmund Kean, the Shakespearian actor, who appeared here several times.

HENRY HALL during a visit to the Norwich Mutual Service Club in February 1938. Broadcaster, band leader and trumpeter, he became director of dance music for the BBC between 1932 and 1937, and later toured Britain with his band until the late 1940s.

VICTOR SYLVESTER (third from left) judging the waltz during a dancing competition at the Thatched Ballroom in the early 1930s.

ANONA WYNN performing at the Hippodrome.

CHARLIE KUNZ AT HIS STEINWAY PIANO, pictured at the Hippodrome.

THE INTERIOR OF THE MADDERMARKET THEATRE in the 1930s. Once a Roman Catholic chapel, it has been the home of the Norwich Players, the amateur repertory company, since 1920.

CLEANING LADIES AT WORK in the old Thatched Ballroom which stood at All Saints' Green until its destruction by a bomb in 1942. In its time it had been the Thatched Cinema, the Thatched Tea Rooms, and the Thatched Theatre.

SCOTT AND WHALEY at the Hippodrome.

THE HAYMARKET PICTURE HOUSE some time before 1920.

SECTION FIVE

Travel

THE EAST ANGLIAN leaving Thorpe station.

A 'BRITANIA' CLASS ENGINE, the most powerful express locomotives ever to run pn the Great Eastern line, carrying the East Anglian nameplate in about 1937. Through trains to London first ran in 1845, the year after Thorpe station opened.

THE EAST ANGLIAN NAMEPLATE in 1937 is fixed to the sleek lines of an LNER 4–6–2 Class A4 engine, of the same class as *Mallard*, the engine that broke the speed record in 1938 by travelling at 126 m.p.h. The streamlined front end was based upon the wedge shape of the French Bugatti railcars. Below, the same engine leaving Thorpe station with five coaches.

THE EAST ANGLIAN, C. 1949, photographed from the railway bridge at the junction of Clarence Road and Carrow Road.

THE EASTERN BELLE in about 1937.

NORWICH HAD THREE STATIONS at one time. Apart from Thorpe station there were Victoria station, opened in 1849 opposite the Norfolk and Norwich hospital, and City station on the old Midland and Great Northern Line, near Heigham Gate. Victoria station was closed to passenger traffic in 1916, and was later destroyed by a bomb in the Second World War. City station closed in 1959.

TRAM NO. 6 TO EARLHAM ROAD. The first recorded public transport in Norwich was a sedan chair that plied for trade in Opie Street, then called Devil's Alley.

THE LAST TRAM ON THE EARLHAM ROAD ROUTE, on 27 July 1935. In 1900 this had been the first tramline to open, and in their first fortnight city trams carried 900,000 passengers. Trams were quite noisy: steel wheels on steel rails usually are.

TAKING THE TRAM TO THE NORFOLK SHOW in 1913. This meant a tram journey to the showground in Eaton Park from Orford Place, shown here with the Lamb Inn on the right. Norwich trams carried a maximum of fifty passengers and ran at intervals of between ten and fifteen minutes. Fares ranged from 1d. to 3d.

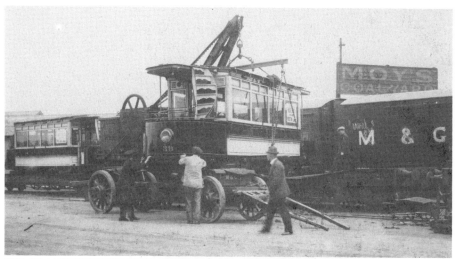

ONE OF A CONSIGNMENT FROM PRESTON, Lancs., Tram No. 39 being unloaded on to a horse-drawn wagon at City station in about 1928. By 1925 some Norwich tram routes had been closed and replaced by motor buses.

AN ARRAY OF CALEY'S CHOCOLATE DELIVERY VEHICLES line up for the camera at their factory near Chapel Field in 1921. On the right are three Leyland vans, the left-hand one with solid tyres, and to its left are two Dennis solid-tyre furniture wagons. A.J. Caley, a local chemist, first produced mineral water, but by the 1880s was producing cocoa and chocolate. In 1932 the firm was bought up by J. Mackintosh and Son Ltd.

THE MOBILE SECTION OF THE NORWICH VOLUNTEERS, 1916, at their headquarters in King Street.

A HEPWORTH'S MODEL T DELIVERY VAN in 1921. In the early 1930s there were fewer than a million cars on the roads, but by 1933 nearly a quarter of a million cars were being produced each year.

THE LODDON TO NORWICH BUS in about 1905.

A NORWICH OMNIBUS in about 1919. This AEC bus with solid tyres, of the type that carried troops in the First World War, is pictured in Recorder Road by Stuart Court. It was only forty years before, in June 1879, that horse-drawn omnibuses had been introduced. These were single-decker buses carrying ten passengers inside and four outside.

A FIRE-ENGINE AT BRAHAMS STORE. This Dennis fire-engine still has solid tyres, retained even after the invention of the pneumatic tyre as punctures were delaying in emergencies and pneumatic tyres were susceptible to coming off on corners after fast driving.

OUTSIDE THE MONUMENT PUBLIC HOUSE, Bedford Street, on a Rowland Grey donkey cart, c. 1905. On the left is the proprietor of the Monument, Sam Hastead, and the man with the cigar is Fred Marris, proprietor of the Boilermakers' Arms.

A MOTLEY CREW OF NORWICH CABBIES c. 1909, when cabbying was evidently not a young man's job.

AN OUTING FROM BEDFORD STREET in about 1909.

SECTION SIX

The Wars

TO THE TANK BANK – a Mark I tank at the Guildhall during Tank Week, 1916, organized to raise public funds for the new wonder weapon. The sign on the right reads 'First buy your bonds then come to the tank', and judging by the queue at the 'investors' entrance' on the left, there was no shortage of takers.

THE ESSEX REGIMENT MUSTER IN THE MARKET PLACE in August 1914.

STANDING AT EASE – some seem more at ease than others.

A REGULATION HAIRCUT under the unfriendly eye of the sergeant on the right.

THE ESSEX REGIMENT, 4 August 1914. In the background is Davey Place, where crowds of onlookers have turned out to watch the proceedings.

ALL OVER THE LAND men were queuing to enlist at the commencement of war. The Essex Regiment shown here formed part of the British Expeditionary Force which landed in France on 12 August. The BEF was practically annihilated at the first battle of Ypres.

THE FEAR OF ATTACK BY ZEPPELINS meant that Norwich soon enforced a night-time blackout. Trains and trams had to travel with blinds drawn, kerbs were whitewashed, and people wore luminous buttons to avoid bumping into one another.

SOON AFTER THE OUTBREAK OF HOSTILITIES trainloads of wounded from Ypres began to arrive and were taken to the Norfolk and Norwich hospital. Over 100,000 Norfolk men fought in the First World War, and one in every nine was killed.

ON THEIR WAY TO THE FRONT in London Street, 4 August 1914, and the postcard seller at the kerb on the right does not miss a last chance to make a sale to a passing soldier.

A 1916 POSTCARD DEPICTING THE EXECUTION OF EDITH CAVELL, the Norwich nurse. She had been arrested by the Germans in 1915, charged with helping British and French soldiers to escape, and was shot.

THE GRAVE OF EDITH CAVELL, lying to the south-east of the cathedral, with its original wooden cross. In 1918 a memorial to her was placed in Tombland.

AN AIR RAID REHEARSAL at St Augustine's School in 1939, when preparations for war were being made up and down the country.

GAS MASKS WERE ISSUED TO ONE AND ALL in case of gas attack, and bleach cream and buckets were left outside chemists shops throughout Norwich.

THE FIRST BOMBS TO FALL ON NORWICH were dropped by two enemy aeroplanes in a raid that lasted only six seconds. Twelve high explosive 250 kg bombs hit Barnards on 9 July 1940 causing three casualties. The resulting fire is shown here. Bombs were then dropped on Colman's, where several were killed, and lastly on Boulton and Paul, where ten lost their lives.

BOULTON AND PAUL'S RIVERSIDE WORKS immediately after four bombs had scored direct hits. Making a huge contribution to the war effort, Boulton and Paul became a prime target whenever Norwich was attacked.

SURREY STREET and the Boar's Head inn, dating from 1495, lies in ruins after the raids of April 1942. During the Second World War, 139 city pubs were damaged or destroyed.

A NEW VIEW OF ST STEPHEN'S CHURCH after the blitz of 1942, when one could see clear across from Surrey Street to St Stephen's church in Rampant Horse Street.

PICKED FROM BAEDECKER'S *BRITISH ISLES* as a place of historic interest, Norwich was selected in April 1942 for two of the *Luftwaffe*'s 'Baedecker Raids', better known to locals as the Norwich blitz. One hundred factories were destroyed and damage to the city centre was severe. Pictured here are two views looking from Surrey Street, showing that the area from there to Rampant Horse Street was completely destroyed.

A NARROW ESCAPE FOR ST JOHN MADDERMARKET, seen here looking across from Exchange Street. Norwich lost seven of its medieval churches during the Second World War, and others were severely damaged.

REDUCED TO RUBBLE – Curls in Orford Place, after the raid of 27/29 April 1942.

ENEMY PLANES SNEAKED IN BEHIND RETURNING BRITISH AIRCRAFT on the night of 5 May 1943, and the anti-aircraft defences had to hold their fire. Phosphorous and explosive incendiary bombs were showered over the city, and one of the victims, Harmers of St Andrew's Street, makers of army uniforms since the First World War is shown here.

THE NORWICH BLITZ WREAKED HAVOC IN THE CITY CENTRE. This was the scene in Rampant Horse Street. Where then Buntings and Woolworths stood gutted is today the site of Marks and Spencer.

THIS BOMB DISPOSAL OFFICER has an unusual use for his handkerchief as he defuses a bomb in Theatre Street. This was one of four bombs that fell on Norwich at five minutes past midnight on the morning of 19 September 1940.

THE BOMB IN THEATRE STREET, a delayed-action thousand pounder, lay there for a week before its removal. It caused great disruption as the whole area had to remain evacuated.

SEVEN PEOPLE WERE INJURED when No. 3 Compass Street (off Ber Street), received a direct hit on the night of 30 July 1940. The row of houses was in such bad condition that Nos 2, 4 and 5 later fell down as well.

AN UNIDENTIFIED STREET after the blitz of 1942.

THE AVENUES after the raids of April 1942, when scenes like this could be seen all over Norwich.

THE SCENE OF DEVASTATION at St Benedict's Gates after one of the 'Baedecker Raids' of 1942.

A LONE DORNIER circled slowly over the city at 6 a.m. on the 30 July 1940. After dropping bombs uselessly into the River Wensum; it selected the bus station for its next target. The resulting explosions flung this double-decker bus across the station, and wrecked another.

GRAPES HILL, on the left, from the Dereham Road in April 1942. Twenty-one houses on the west side of Grapes Hill alone were damaged and at the main junction at the foot of the hill there was an enormous crater.

THE ORCHARD TAVERN in Moutergate Street, after the raid of 2 December 1940. The wife of the licensee and her family were having tea when the bombs fell, but miraculously nobody was hurt. In the same raid, a bomb left a 15 ft crater near the cathedral cloisters, and other bombs fell in the cathedral close.

VAUXHALL STREET, near the Vauxhall Tavern, 18 February 1941, after being hit by what was believed to be a parachute mine.

A PROCESSION OF CIVIC DIGNITARIES makes its way from the City Hall to St Peter Mancroft for a civic service, to the sound of church bells being rung all over Norwich, on VE Day, 8 May 1945.

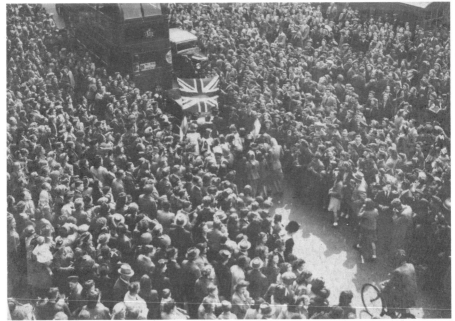

GENTLEMAN'S WALK, VE Day 1945. Later, American Liberators and RAF Mosquitoes, picked out by searchlights, flew over the city dropping coloured flares, as below a conga grew that started on the walk, stretched past and round the Guildhall, and snaked its way back again.

SECTION SEVEN

Around Norwich

THE JUNCTION OF IPSWICH AND NEWMARKET ROADS c. 1906, with tram No. 28 passing the fountain. Today's beleaguered rush-hour motorists might like to reflect a moment upon this scene, pictured at a time when a motor car was quite a rarity.

THE VIEW OVER NORWICH FROM MOUSEHOLD HEATH, where the rebels set up camp during Kett's Rebellion. Seen here in 1936, the castle is on the extreme left, and the short spire of St Peter Mancroft is to its right. The two churches on the far right are St Giles and the Roman Catholic church.

KETT'S REBELLION: In July 1549 Robert Kett led a band of citizens tired of the tyranny of their masters from Wymondham to Norwich, destroying fences and enclosures on their way. Recruits joined the revolt in increasing numbers and soon a small army was approaching Norwich, where the Sheriff attempted to turn them back before he fled after nearly being dragged from his horse.

A camp was established on Mousehold Heath where the army of rebels grew to about 16,000, more than the population of Norwich itself. The city was there for the taking, but Kett instead addressed himself to the task of taking over the government of Norfolk.

The York Herald arrived on 21 July and offered an amnesty, which was refused. The rebel army attacked the city the next morning, but after a short bombardment two figures with white flags approached the gates. Incredibly, they explained they had had no breakfast and asked for a truce so the rebel army could shop for provisions in the city. Permission was refused, the battle resumed, and after initially being repulsed the rebels stormed and took the city.

An unsuccessful attempt was made by the king's forces to retake the city at the end of July, during which Lord Sheffield was dragged from his horse by the wall of St Martin's

PULL'S FERRY, a fifteenth-century watergate, in the 1890s. The lane that leads from it to the cathedral was once a canal along which the stone to build the cathedral was brought.

church, and despite offering any ransom, was clubbed to death. Retribution finally came on 24 August, when the Earl of Warwick arrived with a force of ten thousand, shortly to be augmented by a force of 1,100 German mercenaries, highly trained and battle-hardened veterans. Warwick offered the rebels the choice of surrender and amnesty, or massacre, but again the rebels refused. Warwick quickly took control of the city; that evening forty-nine rebels were hanged and congestion on the gallows was so great that the ladders broke. Next the rebel camp was blockaded and with the arrival of the Germans Kett saw that the game was up and began to retreat.

On 27 August Warwick offered the remaining rebels an amnesty at Dussindale, near Magdalen Gates, but was once more refused. He then delivered his earlier promise: despite placing their chained prisoners before them, the rebels were decimated by a huge volley of shots before being cut down by the cavalry until every man was accounted for. About 3,500 were killed and many hundreds wounded.

Kett managed to escape the battlefield but was captured, tried, found guilty, and confined in the Guildhall. On 7 December 1549, he was taken by hurdle to the castle, where he was bound in chains, hoisted by the neck to a gibbet mounted on the battlements, and left there 'until he should fall down of his own accord'.

THE CUPID AND BOW in about 1910. It stood on the corner of Bishopgate Street, once part of a Roman road that crossed the site of today's city.

BARRACK STREET, once a community of poorly paid shoe workers, took its name from the nearby barracks that stood from 1791 until 1965. On the left is the Windsor Castle public house where J.W. Larkin was the licensee, and on the right a horse and cart waits by the entrance to Bird In Hand Yard. The roof of the Pockthorpe Brewery can just be seen over the houses on the right.

THE VIEW FROM BARRACK STREET TO ST CRISPIN'S ROAD when in 1964, the Prince of Wales public house stood at the junction of Cowgate and Whitefriars.

VANISHED — The Prince of Wales has been demolished to make way for the Magdalen Street flyover, but on the left St James' church still stands, now home of the Norwich Puppet Theatre. This picture was taken in 1975.

THE DEMOLITION OF WHITEFRIARS STREET, 1928. The name dates back to the thirteenth century when the friars who had their monasteries nearby were commonly named after the colour of their habit: Blackfriars, Greyfriars, Whitefriars, etc.

HOW TO LOSE A BRIDGE. Pictured here is the Whitefriars Bridge in 1920, then one of the oldest bridges in Norwich. Needing to be replaced in 1924, it was carefully dismantled and every stone numbered. Placed in the Corporation's care for safekeeping, it simply disappeared and was never seen again. The mystery remained for some years until it was admitted that the stones had been used as a foundation for the then new Aylsham Road.

MAGDALEN STREET was mainly residential in its early years, and was once the home of the Gurneys, Martineaus and Frys. It was the birthplace of Elizabeth Fry, the great prison reformer, who was born in Gurney Court at the north end of the street. It is pictured here in 1900, looking towards Stump Cross.

MAGDALEN STREET, shown here c. 1880, became the shopping centre for the old town on the other side of the river.

CALVERT STREET CONNECTS COLEGATE TO ST CRISPIN'S, and is pictured here in the 1930s, with the Florida Shoe Company on the left. The whole street was destroyed by bombs in the Second World War and only Bacon's House in Colegate survived, though it lost one storey.

COLEGATE AND THE CORNER CAFÉ, 1950 with St Michael-at-Coslany on the left. Colegate, with its fine houses and doorways, and its three churches, was once the home of wealthy wool merchants, later becoming dominated by the shoe industry. John Crome, the Norwich painter, is buried in St George's church on the left.

THE BESS OF BEDLAM, Oak Street, in 1905. Could this be the licensee with his family and employees?

DUCK LANE, now Wellington Lane, had its entrance opposite the Fountain public house in St Benedict's Street. Photographed here in 1937, it was demolished the following year.

THE VIEW OVER ST BENEDICT'S GATES C. 1950, from the City Hall, in the distance on the left, to St Giles' church on the right, its tower the tallest of any Norwich parish church and consequently used as a beacon in Elizabethan times.

ST BENEDICT'S CHURCH, more than a thousand years old, was hit during the Norwich blitz of 1942. The tower was later restored.

THE SMALL SPIRE ON TOP OF ST LAURENCE'S CHURCH, St Benedict's Street, has been a local landmark since the fifteenth century, and marks the top of a stairway that reaches up the tower. It is seen here from along Westwick Street in the 1930s, with the same view below in 1975.

THE IMPOSING TOWER OF THE ROMAN CATHOLIC CHURCH can be seen over twenty miles away. Here, it dominates the view up Grapes Hill in 1973, as a Ford Zephyr turns left on to the Dereham Road.

GRAPES HILL used to be about 12 ft wide, as this 1965 picture shows. This and the photograph above were taken from exactly the same spot.

LOOKING DOWN GRAPES HILL in 1973. The two buildings on the left help to make an accurate comparison with the photograph below.

AN AMBER LIGHT shows at the junction of Grapes Hill and St Giles' Gates in 1964. This picture was taken from the same position as the photograph above.

CHAPEL FIELD ROAD looking towards Grapes Hill, in May 1973. To the right are the Chapel Field Gardens, once ploughed land, later an archery ground, and then a reservoir complete with pumping station. Finally they became the public gardens where Glen Miller played his last concert.

THE SAME SPOT in 1962, only eleven years earlier than the picture above. Compare the last house in the centre of the upper photograph with the house in the centre of the picture below. On the right stands the Drill Hall, built of flint and red brick, which incorporated a tower of the city wall. It was later used for cattle shows and various other exhibitions. On the left, one can see that it was Cup Final and Derby Week.

TWO VIEWS OF COW HILL, above, in 1965 and below, 1975, with Willow Lane on the right and in the background the Alma public house, on the corner of Pottergate. Willow Lane leads to the house where George Borrow once lived. Author of *Lavengro* and *Romany Rye*, he coined the phrase 'Norwich, a fine city'.

POPE'S HEAD YARD, St Peter's Street, in 1953, now the site of the City Hall. Norwich had many of these 'yards', often with families crowded together in insanitary conditions. In one recorded instance 11 families, 34 people in all, lived in just one house. Squalor and overcrowding had existed at least since the reign of Elizabeth I, and in 1850 Norwich still had large numbers of poor living in congested conditions. Then, a fifth of the population were paupers, and a report of 1844 found everywhere a 'total lack of hygiene'. At this time the water supply was 'bad in quantity, bad in quality, and bad in everything that should constitute a water supply'. Many city houses were totally without drainage, and their liquid refuse, when not poured into a cesspit, simply lay in the street and stagnated. About 3,000 of the city's 18,000 houses had water closets, but even these emptied into the river Wensum which became 'thoroughly polluted, presenting all the features of a large sewer'. Overcrowding extended even to churchyards, where bones and fragments of skeletons often lay scattered on the ground.

SECTION EIGHT

A Last Look

THE NORWICH RADIO SOCIETY in 1921 on an outing to Ringland, proudly displaying on the right their state-of-the-art Amplion Concert Dragon radio, with oak trumpet. In the centre is a Crystavox crystal set extension speaker, and the whole apparatus would have been powered by a nearby 'accumulator'.

POOLE'S MYRIORAMAS advertise their show at a time when apparently 95,000 families were using Wright's 'Eureka' gas cookers. On the centre left, it seems that 'Resurrection Morn' was due even in 1895 when this picture of a Norwich advertising hoarding was taken.

'DIRECT FROM THE TEA GARDENS TO THE TEAPOT' – Lipton's Teas and other posters in 1895.

AN EVERYDAY SCENE BY THE ROYAL HOTEL in about 1905. Prince of Wales Road is to the right, while in front of the Royal Hotel tram No. 36 to Aylsham Road makes its way through Agricultural Hall Plain.

THE NAVY LEAGUE was founded in 1913, in order that boys 'might be trained in the rudiments of seamanship and acquire a taste for ocean life'. Shown here is their first training ship, the Lowestoft sailing trawler *Elsie*, purchased in 1912, and renamed the *Lord Nelson*. It was replaced in 1938 by the ex-paddle-steamer *Glengary* and in 1946 the Admiralty loaned a motor torpedo boat, pictured below by the Great Eastern Hotel (now the Hotel Nelson) in 1963.

THE OLD CARROW BRIDGE used to stand opposite Carrow Hill a little further along the river than the present bridge, and is shown here c. 1910 with a Thames-type wherry in the foreground and Colman's factory behind.

THE RAILWAY BRIDGE OVER STOKE ROAD at the bottom of Long John Hill, pictured in 1930.

THE RESIDENTS OF GLOBE YARD, Heigham Street, including some Morrisons, Sweatmans and Waseys, photographed possibly after a visit by Marie Lloyd during the First World War, while all the menfolk of the yard were serving in the forces. In the centre the two ladies holding babies look as though they are related while behind them the lady with the very individual hairstyle gives a big grin for the camera.

THE JENNY LIND HOSPITAL in the early 1920s. Jenny Lind, 'the Swedish nightingale', was a soprano who became famous in the mid-1800s and made many bequests to charity. Here, at the Jenny Lind Hospital, a boy undergoes some rather fearsome looking tests.

THE NORWICH AMATEUR BICYCLE CLUB C. 1920. In the photograph are Mr Charles Willmott, and seated centre with the stick, Mr Rumsey Wells, the internationally known Norwich cap-maker.

FIVE GO BICYCLING — members of the Amateur Bicycle Club set off around the Norwich recreation track on a five-man tandem in 1921.

A PRESENT FROM THE *LUFTWAFFE*, photographed in a Norwich garden during the Second World War.

CHAPEL FIELD GARDENS in 1938/9, after work had started on the **ARP** shelters.

GOING TO ANY LENGTHS to attract publicity, Kirk's Garage at St Faith's evidently went one length further during the jubilee of 1935.

DEMOLISHED – the word appears so often throughout this book. Shown here in the 1930s is Wellington Lane, once Duck Lane, off St Giles', pulled down to make way for the Grapes Hill developments.

'VICE AND ASSISTANCE OBTAINABLE IMMED-IATELY'. A Norwich police call box in the 1930s.

'THE MOST EXPENSIVE CAP-MAKER IN THE WORLD', Mr H. Rumsey-Wells, in his own words. Internationally known, he always carried a monocle and snuff box until his death in 1937.

MRS SWIRES AND HER DUCK, which apparently would follow her anywhere.

SWAIN'S PHOTOGRAPHIC SHOP, 27 St Giles' Street, half boarded up in April 1942 against the threat of blast damage. It was nevertheless hit by a bomb only days later, when the next-door Hippodrome received a direct hit and four people were killed.

PEOPLE WERE ENCOURAGED TO PRACTICE WEARING THEIR GAS MASKS for fifteen minutes every week in 1940. Here, George Swain's daughter Judy and her companion try on theirs.

GEORGE SWAIN, who took many of the photographs in this book, and from whose collection all the pictures come. After an apprenticeship with Lafayette in London, he returned to Norwich aged sixteen to work in his parents' photographic shop. In the early 1920s he became a pioneer of aerial photography, often having to stand in open cockpits to get his pictures. He later risked his life to get his pictures of the Norwich blitz, cycling to the scenes of newly wrought devastation with his Super Ikonta camera. His collection of photographs of Norwich is comprehensive, despite having to destroy over a quarter of a million negatives in 1933 due to lack of space. He retired in 1974, and died in 1981.

ACKNOWLEDGEMENTS

This book owes its existence to the kind help and support generously given by Judy Ball, who lent all the photographs from the collection of her father, George Swain. Her collection has been used many times but never so extensively as I have done, and for this I am extremely grateful.

Thanks are due to the Norwich Local Studies Library, who unfailingly helped.

Special thanks to Antonia Macgregor for her additional research.